James McNair's
SALMON
COOKBOOK

Photography by Patricia Brabant
CHRONICLE BOOKS · SAN FRANCISCO

Printed in Japan

Library of Congress
Cataloging-in Publication Data
McNair, James K.
James McNair's Salmon Cookbook
/ James McNair ;
photography by Patricia Brabant.
p. cm.
Includes index.
ISBN 0-87701-478-7
ISBN 0-87701-453-1 (pbk.)
1. Cookery (Salmon) I. Title.
TX748.S24N36 1987
641.6'92—dc19
87-17382 CIP

Distributed in Canada by
Raincoast Books
112 East Third Avenue
Vancouver, British Columbia V5T 1C8

10 9 8 7 6 5 4

Chronicle Books
San Francisco, California

To the Cotton clan, my adopted California family—Aylett and Maggie, and
Julie Cotton; Gail and Tad, Ken "Trip" III, Tanya, and Misty High; and
Kristi and Bob, Alex, Brooksley, Jody, Kimberley, Poco, and Samantha
Spence—with appreciation for their love and assistance through the ups
and downs of my professional and personal life, and for making me feel like
family.

And in memory of the matriarch, Martha Jane Cotton, my good friend and
confidant, who made life at The Rockpile possible.

Produced by The Rockpile Press, San Francisco and Lake Tahoe

Art direction, photographic and food styling, and book design
by James McNair

Editorial production assistance by Lin Cotton

Studio kitchen assistance by Gail High

Photography assistance by Sheryl Scott

Typography and mechanical production by Cleve Gallat and Peter Linato
of Chuck Thayer Associates, Ltd.

CONTENTS

A PRIZED CATCH   5

POACHED, STEAMED, & SIMMERED   13

BAKED, ROASTED, & SAUTÉED   27

GRILLED, BARBECUED, & BROILED   41

SMOKED & CURED   53

COOKED SALMON   69

SAUCES & SEASONINGS   83

Index   94

Acknowledgments   96

A PRIZED CATCH

Salmon has long enjoyed well-deserved regard among gourmets as one of life's great delicacies. Ironically, it's also popular with the general public, who usually prefer beef to fish. Even those who claim to dislike fish in general often appreciate salmon.

Salmon fanciers can feast on their favorite fish year-round. The season for all the various species only runs from May through fall, but farm-raised salmon is always available. Fresh salmon is easily purchased near harvest areas and is occasionally shipped to other parts of the country. More often, though, it is "fresh frozen" before transport. Smoked, cured, or canned salmon accounts for much of the salmon eaten away from the coastal markets and can fulfill the cravings for this delectable fish whenever and wherever it can't be found fresh.

The salmon catch is the most valuable segment of the fishing industry that stretches from Central California's Pacific coast and interior rivers north to Alaska. Some of the same species found in these areas range as far away as Japan. Atlantic salmon, once a staple of the eastern seaboard, has virtually disappeared from American waters as a result of overfishing. The East now receives most of its fresh salmon from Nova Scotia, or flies it in from northern Europe or the West Coast.

LIFE CYCLE

The journey of young salmon begins with a swim, often quite treacherous, from their birthplace in freshwater rivers or lakes to the ocean, where they undergo biochemical changes that allow them to live in salt water for several years. Then one spring instinct sends the firm, fattened fish swimming upriver, sometimes thousands of miles, to the quiet inland place of their birth. All this in spite of floods, rapids, dams, and countless predators. The survivors mate, spawn, then die of exhaustion from their perilous trek. In a short time, their fingerlings begin the cycle all over again.

Species

HEALTHY OILS

For a long time, those who love salmon had been warned to go easy on it and other fatty fish that are high in cholesterol. Happily, the entire nutrition picture has changed in recent years. Salmon and other fish that develop in cold water are now acknowledged to contain a higher proportion of polyunsaturated omega-3 fatty acids than their lean warmer water relatives.

Omega-3 has come to the attention of health and medical professionals because it appears to lower blood cholesterol levels, thereby aiding in the prevention of strokes and heart attacks. Studies reported in medical journals reveal that these fatty oils may also help stave off a host of other conditions, including arthritis and breast cancer. All of these findings are great news for salmon fanciers.

In addition to being rich in protein and to containing a good balance of phosphorus and calcium needed to prevent bone deterioration, salmon is a good source of vitamin D.

The flesh of the salmon you catch or find in the market can vary in color from deep red to nearly white, according to species, eating habits, age, and habitat. In general, the East Coast salmon is paler than its West Coast counterpart.

The Chinook, also known as the king or spring salmon, is the most prized Pacific species. This is truly the king of all the salmon, not only in flavor but also in size; it ranges from 6 to more than 100 pounds, though the average is around 20 pounds. To identify Chinooks, look for black lower gums and skin that is dark blue or blue green along the dorsal region, fading to silver on the sides and belly. Black spots dot the back and tail. Their flesh ranges from red to almost white. Chinooks, which have life spans from four to seven years, are found from the delta rivers of northern California to the far northern waters of Alaska.

Coho, or silver, salmon look and taste much like Chinooks, but are smaller, from four to ten pounds, due to their shorter life-span of about three years. The coho's gums are white and it has fewer black spots and darker flesh than the Chinook. Farmed-raised cohos average about one pound, perfect for individual servings. They swim as far south as the Monterey area of California and as far north as the Bering Sea between Alaska and Siberia.

Sockeye salmon is less fatty than the preceding two more highly regarded catches. This species, which is sometimes called red or blueback salmon, is distinguished by its huge glassy eyes and spotless blue green dorsal area. The flesh is dark red and firmer in texture than Chinook or coho. When sockeyes return to freshwater, in which they can live up to a year, they turn deep red with green black heads. This species is mainly used for canning. Home stretches from northern California up to Alaska.

Pink, or humpbacked, salmon have a life expectancy of only two years. They average just five pounds, which makes them the smallest species harvested from Pacific waters, and are much less fatty than their fellow salmon. Large oval spots cover the dorsal area and tail and males have a prominent cartilaginous dorsal hump. As the common name implies, the flesh is pale pink. Like sockeyes, pinks mostly end up in cans. They are found from the rivers of northern California all the way to Asia.

Chum, or dog, salmon weigh in at eight to ten pounds, though some get larger. They look much like an outsized version of the sockeye. Their coarse-textured flesh shades from pink to white and has little fatty oil. During spawning season, they develop elongated teeth; hence the "dog" name. The species is very prolific in extreme northern Alaskan and Asian waters.

Atlantic salmon are now found upward from Maine and across to the waters north of Europe. Although salmon caught off Scandinavia have weighed up to 100 pounds, the species averages 15 to 25 pounds, with much smaller farm-raised specimens available. These are the fish known as Nova Scotia, Scottish, Irish, or Norwegian salmon. Their spot-covered dorsal area is dark blue green, fading to silver all over. The flesh is paler than that of their Pacific cousins. Some ichthyologists claim that Atlantic salmon are more closely related to steelhead trout than to the various species of salmon found in the Pacific.

Those concerned about the concentration of chemical contaminants in fish fat should be relieved to know that continual government monitoring of the salmon industry assures that the fish being marketed come from clean waters.

With these facts in mind, indulge in salmon as often as you like without guilt.

Catching and Cleaning

DOGS BEWARE

Salmon from the Pacific Northwest region may host *rickettsia*, a microorganism which can prove fatal to 50 to 90 percent of dogs who become infected from eating parasite-infested raw or undercooked species of the salmon and trout family. Symptoms usually appear within five to 12 days of ingestion; watch for depression, lethargy, loss of appetite, increased temperature, enlarged lymph nodes, vomiting, and diarrhea. When detected in time, the lives of most dogs can be saved through veterinary treatment.

To prevent the possibility of contamination, dispose of all salmon trimmings, including skin, in a dog-proof container. When traveling in areas where dogs may come in contact with dead fish, keep your pet on a leash.

Properly cooked salmon poses no threat to our canine friends.

The very best salmon is the one you hook yourself. Only a few hours should pass between the catch and the cooking for the fullest flavor. As soon as the fish is out of the water, kill it with a sharp blow to the head, then make a small deep cut behind the anal opening and drain off as much blood as you can. Even at this point, the digestive enzymes will continue to work, causing the fish to spoil, so clean the salmon immediately, if possible, and place it on ice. If this is inconvenient, place it on ice and clean it within a couple of hours.

To clean a salmon, place it on a cutting board large enough to hold the entire fish comfortably. If the catch is too big for available boards, cover a kitchen counter or other surface with several thicknesses of newspaper and top them with butcher paper or white freezer wrap. Lay the fish down on its side with the stomach facing you. Insert a small sharp knife in the anal opening and cut along the middle of the stomach all the way to the head. Be careful not to pierce the entrails as you cut. Spread the cavity open and pull out and discard the viscera, or entrails. Using a spoon, locate, remove, and discard the black kidney lodged along the backbone. Now, if you are cleaning a female, look for a sack of brightly colored roe; it will be there if the time of year is right. Remove this delicacy and place it on ice.

Cut off and discard the fins. Using a special scaling knife or the dull side of a butcher knife, remove the scales by scraping along the skin from the tail toward the head. There is no need to scale the fish, however, when it is simply going to be skinned and filleted.

If you plan to cook the fish whole, you will probably want to leave the head and tail intact for a showy presentation. If not, remove the head by positioning the knife behind the pectoral fins (the fins at the base of the head) and cutting along the bone that protects the gill openings. Finally, cut through the backbone and dispose of the head or save it for making fish stock. Cut off the tail at the point just above where it joins the body.

Position the fish in the sink, tail end up. Wash the fish very thoroughly but quickly under cold running water. Pat dry with paper toweling before cooking, cutting up, or storing as described later.

Shopping

Since catching your own fish isn't always possible, you must rely on the fish market or supermarket. The fish are sold whole, dressed (cleaned), or pan-dressed (cleaned with head and tail removed); cut into large chunks, or roasts; sliced crosswise into steaks; and as boned sides, or fillets, whole or in pieces.

Careful inspection will reveal whether salmon advertised as fresh actually meets that description. When shopping for a whole fish, never buy one that has not already been cleaned, no matter how fresh the salesperson assures you it is. Any fish should have been cleaned sooner than the time it takes to reach retail shelves.

Begin the check with your nose. Fresh salmon should have a mild odor; if it smells fishy, pass it by. Unfortunately, cut-up salmon is often sold prewrapped in plastic. When you have no choice but to buy from such a source, be sure the source is reliable, and don't hesitate to return the fish immediately upon opening if it has a foul odor.

The skin of a fresh salmon is shiny; that of a fish past its prime is dull. Any fat that shows along the edges of the skin side of steaks or fillets should be pink, never brown from oxidation, an indication that the fish has been kept too long.

Next check the scales, if they are still intact; they should have a bright silvery cast and glisten in the light. If a fish has not been scaled by the supplier and more than a few scales are missing, it's a sign that it was improperly handled at some point enroute to the market and should be avoided. Likewise pass up salmon with gills that are turning either brown or light colored; they should be deep red. Eyes should protrude and be bright and clear, with shiny dark pupils.

Salmon flesh that is fresh will be firm and elastic and spring back when pressed with a fingertip. It will also cling tightly to the bone. Look inside the stomach cavity of whole fish to be sure it is smooth. Pass up those with any trace of blood or entrails or with bones that separate easily from the flesh, soft flesh, or darkening areas. Rough texturing of the membrane along the ribs, known as belly burn, indicates that the entrails were pierced during cleaning, causing stomach enzymes to leak and begin breaking down flesh.

SALMON CAVIAR

In the truest sense of the word, caviar can be prepared only from the eggs (roe) of sturgeon. But the roe of salmon makes a good caviarlike product, which we simply call caviar in the same way that we call sparkling wines champagne. Salmon roe is large in comparison to that of sturgeon and the color varies from bright red to light orange.

Salmon caviar is sold fresh in bulk or pasteurized in jars. Whichever way you buy it, store it in the coldest spot of the refrigerator or, preferably, on ice. Once opened, transfer fresh caviar or vacuum-packed caviar to airtight containers as long as 2 or 3 days for fresh, or up to 5 days for pasteurized. Turn pasteurized caviar into a fine strainer and rinse under gently flowing cool water for 2 or 3 minutes. Drain, cover, and chill before serving.

The brilliantly colored caviar makes a stunning garnish. It is also good served on thin black bread or toasted white bread. Offer a variety of condiments: lemon juice, sour cream, minced hard-cooked egg, chopped onion or chives, and fresh dill.

Storing and Cooking

CUTTING UP

You can expect a dressed whole salmon to yield about 67 percent boned edible meat. As a general guide, a 9-pound dressed fish yields a dozen 6-ounce steaks, or 2 whole 3-pound fillets, each of which can be sliced into 6 equal portions. In other words, the fish serves 12.

To cut steaks, slice the fish crosswise into equal widths, usually ¾ to 1¼ inches are desirable. For smaller appetites, divide steaks in half by cutting along either side of the dorsal bone (discard the bone).

To cut a pan-dressed salmon into whole fillets, insert a knife at the head end of the fish with the blade parallel to the backbone. Cut the fish in two by slicing along the backbone to the tail end, leaving the backbone attached to one side. Now remove the backbone by slipping the knife under it at the head end and cutting along the bone to the tail end. Cut off fins and trim away bony ridges. If you wish to remove the skin, place the fillet skin side down on a firm surface and cut it away with a sharp knife.

To divide whole fillets into individual servings, cut into pieces on the diagonal to balance out the thin tail section with the fleshier center portion, thereby producing pieces of uniform thickness.

Rinse fresh salmon quickly under cold running water and pat dry with paper toweling. It is then ready for cooking or storing.

If you must store the salmon, tightly enclose the rinsed and dried fish in plastic wrap and keep it in the coldest part of the refrigerator for no more than two days. For longer storage, freeze fresh fish as soon as you get it home.

To freeze your own fresh salmon, place steaks or fillets in heavy-duty plastic freezer bags or containers and add cold water to immerse the fish completely. Or tightly wrap whole fish or pieces in moistureproof plastic or foil, pressing the wrap to eliminate as much air as possible. Date the package and position it in an uncrowded area in the freezer. Flavor is best if the fish is cooked within two months, though it can be frozen for up to four months.

The only way to secure unsmoked or uncured salmon in many places is to buy it already frozen. When you purchase frozen salmon, be sure the label reads "fresh frozen," which means that when the fish was killed it was immediately bled, cleaned, and flash-frozen. Packages should be frost-free; frost is a telltale sign that temperature changes have occurred during storage or that the fish has been around too long. The flesh should not be discolored or appear dried out. The entire fish should be frozen solid; there must be no soft spots. If you buy frozen salmon and wish to keep it frozen, place it in the home freezer as soon as possible; it must not thaw even slightly.

Most states require that retail packages containing fish that has been previously frozen and is being sold thawed to be labeled accordingly. It is unsafe to ever refreeze fish. You can, however, refreeze salmon once it has been cooked.

To thaw frozen salmon, place the unopened package in a bowl in the refrigerator until defrosted. Bacteria grow too rapidly to thaw fish at room temperature. When the salmon has defrosted, quickly rinse and dry it, as you would fresh fish. Thawed fish should be used within twenty-four hours.

Follow the preparation directions and cooking times suggested in the individual recipes. For far too long recipes have instructed readers to flake the fish with a fork to test for doneness. Of course, what constitutes perfectly cooked fish is a matter of personal taste, but for me—and for a lot of other good professional and home cooks—the fish is overcooked by the time it flakes easily. A better indication of doneness is to note the point at which the flesh changes from translucent to opaque. It is preferable to have the fish still a little bright pink or red near the bone or center than to have it dried out and tasteless from overcooking. To test for opaqueness, insert a sharp knife into the thickest part of the fish and gently pry the meat apart so you can see the flesh. Another method is to insert a slender wooden skewer into the fish at the thickest part; the fish is ready if the skewer meets very little resistance as it enters.

I have grouped the recipes according to cooking method. In the Cooked Salmon section the dishes call for already cooked fish, which can be arrived at by any of the cooking methods in the book. Look to this section for innovative ways to use up tasty, expensive leftovers.

At the end of the book I've included a number of sauces to accompany hot or cold salmon. Although there are specific sauces suggested in some of the recipes in the other sections, feel free to pair cooking methods and sauces according to your own taste.

Most of my recipes are in keeping with Escoffier's directive, and my own preference, to prepare salmon simply. For the sake of special entertaining or just plain fun for the cook, I've added a few complex preparations.

BONING

There are times when you will want to bone a whole salmon or salmon chunk for stuffing. To remove the bones from a dressed salmon or salmon section, lay the fish on its side and with a sharp, flexible knife, extend the opening of the cavity from the base of the head to the beginning of the tail. Next, insert the blade in the cavity at the head end, with the blade resting on top of and perpendicular to the backbone. Cut along the top side of the backbone to the tail end, stopping just short of the tail and being careful not to cut through the flesh and skin along the back of the fish. Turn the fish over, insert the knife in the cavity in the same manner, and again cut along the bone from the head to the tail end. Now cut through the backbone inside the cavity where it joins the head and where it joins the tail. Gently pull the backbone from the cavity, using the knife as necessary to free it. Pull out any remaining bones with tweezers.

Poached, Steamed, & Simmered

*E*arly in the season salmon have particularly delicate texture and flavor, which make them especially suited to cooking in liquid. Use plain water, water and wine with herbs and lemon added, milk, or the traditional poaching stock known as court bouillon. Whole fish, fillets, and steaks may all be poached in the same way, either on the stovetop or in a 375° F. oven.

Steaming is a very healthful way to prepare tender salmon, as the addition of cooking fats is not necessary. At the same time, the naturally high fat content of salmon itself releases an intense flavor in the steaming process.

Both poaching and steaming are ideal ways to prepare fish that will be used in recipes calling for cooked salmon.

Concluding this section are two simmered soups: a hearty chowder that couples salmon and corn and a velvety rich bisque.

Cold Poached Whole Salmon

About 3 quarts Poaching Liquid
(page 84)
1 whole 6- to 10-pound salmon,
dressed and boned (page 11)
if desired
Salt
Freshly ground white pepper
3 or 4 lemons, very thinly sliced
(optional)
1 or 2 bunches fresh young sorrel,
shredded (optional)
½ pound fresh mushrooms, thinly
sliced (optional)
Lemon Aspic (page 93)
Fresh herbs such as dill, lemon thyme,
parsley, or tarragon for garnish
Pesticide-free edible flowers such as
borage or nasturtium for garnish
(optional)

A decorated whole salmon is the star of any buffet table. If you do not have a poacher specially designed to hold a whole fish, improvise with a roasting pan, shallow metal tub, or any heat-resistant container with a lid that will accommodate the fish completely immersed in simmering liquid. Lacking an adequately sized pan, cut the fish in half crosswise, cook the halves separately, reassemble the fish on the serving tray, and conceal the cut with the coating or decorations.

The preceding pages show two presentations: one depicts the recipe, coated with lemon-flavored aspic, decorated with flowers, and served with the cucumber variation of Sour Cream Sauce (page 91); the other illustrates the variation, covered with Herbed Mayonnaise (page 90) and cucumber slices. In either case, you may stuff the fish with sorrel, lemons, and mushrooms for added flavor; serve the stuffing along with the fish.

Pour the Poaching Liquid into a large fish poacher and bring to a simmer over medium heat. Reduce the heat to keep the liquid at a simmer.

Remove the fins from the salmon, then quickly rinse the fish in cold running water and pat dry with paper toweling. Season lightly with salt and pepper. If desired, stuff the cavity of the salmon with the lemons, sorrel, and mushrooms. To determine the cooking time, measure the fish across the back (hold the ruler perpendicular to the spine) at its widest point. Wrap the fish tightly in several layers of cheesecloth and tie with white cotton string in several places along the length of the salmon to prevent the fish from falling apart and to keep the stuffing intact during cooking and removal from the pan. If you do not have a fish poacher with a removable rack, leave sufficient excess cloth at either end of the fish or make folds in the cloth along the top of the fish to act as handles for lifting. Place the fish on the poaching rack and gently lower it into the pan. If you have formed cheesecloth handles on either end, drape them over the top of the fish. If the liquid does not cover the fish, add enough boiling water to cover completely. Bring the liquid to a boil, then reduce the heat to low, cover, and gently simmer the fish 10 minutes per inch of thickness. Do not let the liquid boil; there should be only a few bubbles breaking on the surface.

Using the handles of the poaching rack or the cheesecloth handles, carefully lift the fish from the poaching liquid to a large tray and remove the cheesecloth. Position the fish on its side on the tray. Very carefully peel off the skin and remove and discard any cartilage and excess fat. Scrape off any gray flesh with a dull knife and use tweezers to pull out any exposed bones. Turn fish over and peel and clean other side. Wrap salmon tightly in plastic wrap and refrigerate until very cold.

To decorate, carefully place the fish on a wire rack set on a shallow-rimmed tray. Arrange the garnishes on the fish to determine desired pattern, then set the decorations aside. Spoon a thin layer of the thickened aspic over the fish and gently brush with a feather brush, if necessary, to achieve a smooth, glossy coating. Grasp the decorations with tweezers, dip them into the liquid aspic, and place them on the salmon in the selected pattern. Refrigerate the salmon, uncovered, until the layer of aspic sets up, about 15 minutes.

Remove the salmon from the refrigerator and cover with a second layer of aspic, coating the decorations as well. It may be necessary to repeat with several layers of aspic, chilling for about 15 minutes between each application, to cover the fish and decorations completely. The salmon may be served as soon as the final coat of aspic is set or it may be covered with a foil tent (don't allow it to touch the aspic) and refrigerated for several hours before serving.

Serves 8 to 14.

VARIATION: After removing the skin, carefully and evenly mask the salmon, except for the head and tail, with Herbed Mayonnaise (page 90). Beginning at the tail end, arrange paper-thin slices of unpeeled English (seedless) cucumber over the entire fish in an overlapping scale pattern. Garnish with fresh herbs and flowers and serve with additional Herbed Mayonnaise.

Poached Fillet or Steaks

1 to 2 quarts Poaching Liquid,
    (page 84) or other liquid
    (see introduction)
1½ pounds salmon fillet, skinned and
    cut into 4 equal pieces, or 4 steaks
    (about 6 ounces *each*)

Cook salmon pieces in plain water, part water and part wine, or, preferably, the more flavorful Poaching Liquid on page 84. To eliminate the central bone in a steak, divide the steak into two pieces by cutting along either side of the bone and then discarding the bone. Cut away and discard the skin. Form the two pieces into one disk by interlocking them, wrapping the small end of each half around the large center section of the other half. Secure with toothpicks before wrapping each piece in cheesecloth, tying with string, and poaching. Serve both regular lemon-flavored Hollandaise Sauce (page 87) and its avocado variation with the warm fillets.

Heat the liquid in a saucepan over medium heat until simmering.

Quickly rinse the salmon under cold running water and pat dry with paper toweling. If using the reassembled steaks described in the introduction and shown in the photo, wrap each portion in cheesecloth and tie with white cotton string to keep the fish intact during cooking. It is not necessary to wrap whole steaks or pieces of fillet. Place the fish in a flameproof dish or skillet. Pour the simmering liquid over the fish to cover completely and place the pan over medium heat until fish is done, 2 to 3 minutes for thin pieces, up to 10 minutes for thick steaks. Do not allow the liquid to boil during the cooking; there should be only a few bubbles breaking on the surface. With a slotted spatula, remove the cooked salmon immediately to paper toweling to drain briefly. Remove cheesecloth and toothpicks, if used. Spoon some of each sauce on individual plates, then top with the salmon, and serve immediately.

Serves 4.

VARIATION: To serve cold, drain poached fish as directed, then wrap well and refrigerate for at least 1 hour or as long as overnight. Serve with Herbed Mayonnaise (page 90) or other cold sauce in place of the pair of warm hollandaise sauces.

Steamed Salmon

6 salmon steaks (about 6 ounces *each*),
    or 2¼ pounds fillet, skinned and
    cut into 6 equal pieces
½ white onion, thinly sliced and
    separated into rings
About 6 fresh young sorrel leaves,
    shredded, or 6 fresh dill sprigs
6 fresh parsley sprigs
Juice of 1 or 2 limes
Salt
Freshly ground white pepper
Whole fresh young sorrel leaves
    for garnish
Wild mustard or other edible flowers
    for garnish

Salmon steaks or fillets come out beautifully using this technique. They can be served warm with Sorrel Cream (page 87) or cold with Rémoulade Sauce (page 92). As a general guide for steaming salmon, measure the fish at its thickest part, then allow about nine minutes for each inch of thickness.

Pour about 2 inches of water into the pan of a large steamer, place over medium heat, and bring to a boil.

Quickly rinse the salmon under cold running water and pat dry with paper toweling. Arrange the salmon on a shallow dish that will fit on the steamer rack with about 1-inch clearance between the dish and rack sides. Top the fish with onion rings, shredded sorrel or dill sprigs, and parsley. Sprinkle with lime juice, salt, and pepper to taste. Set the dish on the rack positioned over the simmering water, cover the steamer, and cook until the fish is just opaque, 6 to 10 minutes. Remove the fish from the steamer, discard the onion and herbs, and carefully remove and discard the skin from the steaks. To serve hot, arrange the salmon on dinner plates, spoon on some of the sauce, garnish, and serve immediately. To serve cold, cover and refrigerate steamed salmon for up to several hours. Garnish the cold salmon and serve the sauce on the side.

Serves 6.

VARIATION: To create a decorative woven presentation, cut a single serving portion of salmon fillet of uniform thickness into 10 equal strips. Place 5 of the strips side by side on a flat plate that will fit on the steamer rack. Working with the remaining strips one at a time, interlace them with the strips on the plate, alternating the pattern as you add the next strip, to form a woven look. Repeat with remaining fillet portions. Steam as above. Serve warm or cold on top of a selected sauce.

Salmon and Corn Chowder

By all means use corn cut fresh from the cob if possible, although canned or frozen kernels are satisfactory.

Melt the butter in a large saucepan over low heat. Add the leeks and cook, stirring frequently, until very soft but not browned, about 8 minutes.

Add the potato to the leeks and stir to coat with the butter. Pour in the stock and simmer uncovered over low heat for 15 minutes. Add the milk and cream and simmer for 10 minutes more. Add the salmon and corn and simmer just until the fish and corn are done, about 5 minutes. Season to taste with salt and pepper. Serve immediately.

Serves 8.

3 tablespoons unsalted butter
2 medium-sized leeks, including tender green portion, cut into very thin julienne
1 large potato, peeled and cut into small dice
2 cups Fish Stock (page 84) or bottled clam juice
3 cups milk
3 cups heavy (whipping) cream
1 pound salmon fillet, skinned, rinsed, dried, and cut into small dice
1 cup whole kernel corn, preferably white
Salt
Freshly ground black or white pepper

Salmon Bisque

1 tablespoon saffron threads, or 1 teaspoon powdered saffron (optional)
¾ cup heavy (whipping) cream
4 tablespoons (½ stick) unsalted butter
6 tablespoons minced shallots or green onions, white portion only
6 tablespoons unbleached all-purpose flour
1 tablespoon tomato paste
4½ cups Fish Stock (page 84), homemade chicken stock, or canned chicken broth, preferably low-sodium
1 pound salmon fillet, skinned, rinsed, dried, and coarsely chopped
3 egg yolks
Salt
Ground cayenne pepper
1 teaspoon freshly squeezed lemon juice, or to taste
Fresh whole chives or parsley leaflets, preferably flat-leaf Italian type, for garnish
Pesticide-free garlic or onion flowers for garnish (optional)

Serve small portions of this smooth rich soup to begin a special meal.

In a small bowl, stir the saffron into the cream and set aside.

Melt the butter in a large saucepan over medium heat. Add the shallots or green onions and sauté until soft but not browned, about 3 minutes. Using a wire whisk or wooden spoon, blend in the flour and cook, stirring, until bubbly, about 2 minutes. Quickly stir in the tomato paste. Gradually pour in the stock, whisking it into the flour until the mixture is thick and smooth, about 10 minutes. Add the salmon, reduce the heat to low, partially cover, and simmer until the salmon falls apart, about 15 minutes.

Transfer the soup to a food processor or blender and purée until smooth. Then pour it through a fine wire sieve into a large bowl, pressing the salmon with the back of a wooden spoon to force as much through as possible. Discard whatever remains in the sieve.

Pour the strained soup into a clean saucepan. Whisk together the egg yolks and saffron-flavored cream and then whisk in about ½ cup of the soup. Whisk the yolk mixture into the remaining soup and place the pan over medium heat. Cook, whisking constantly, until the soup almost comes to a boil. Season to taste with salt, cayenne pepper, and lemon juice. Strain again through a fine sieve. Reheat, ladle into individual bowls, garnish, and serve immediately. If desired, transfer to a covered container and refrigerate as long as overnight. Reheat gently just before serving, stirring to prevent the bisque from boiling.

Serves 6 to 8.

BAKED, ROASTED, & SAUTÉED

*B*aking and roasting are probably the easiest ways to cook salmon. There's no grill to scrub or poaching liquid to prepare. Just combine the fish with seasonings and pop it into the oven while you go on with preparing the rest of the meal.

Following several oven-cooked salmon dishes is a recipe that demonstrates the potential for sautéing. Use it as a guide for creating other quick-and-easy salmon presentations.

Parchment-Wrapped Salmon

6 20-inch squares of baking
    parchment or heavy-duty
    butcher paper
Safflower or other vegetable oil
2 small carrots, peeled and cut into
    very thin julienne
2 medium-sized leeks, or 4 green
    onions, including tender green
    portion, cut into very thin
    julienne
1 large red sweet pepper,
    cut into very thin julienne
6 salmon steaks (4 to 6 ounces *each*),
    or 1½ pounds fillet, skinned and
    cut into 6 equal pieces
6 tablespoons dry white wine
6 tablespoons freshly squeezed lime
    or lemon juice
3 tablespoons unsalted butter, melted
Salt
Freshly ground black pepper
6 thin lime or lemon slices
24 fresh basil, chervil, cilantro
    (coriander), dill, parsley, or
    tarragon sprigs

Aromatic bursts delight diners when these puffed packets are cut open with a sharp knife. Be sure the rest of the meal is ready so the packets can go directly from the oven to the table.

Preheat the oven to 475° F.

Cut the parchment or butcher paper into heart-shaped pieces, using the full width of the paper. Rub one side of each heart lightly with vegetable oil and set aside.

Blanch the carrot, leek or green onion, and red pepper strips in boiling water until crisp-tender, about 1 minute. Cool in ice water and drain well; dry on paper toweling. When dry, distribute most of the vegetables equally over one-half of the oiled side of each piece of parchment, leaving a 1-inch border. Quickly rinse the salmon under cold running water and pat dry with paper toweling. Top the vegetables with a piece of salmon.

Combine the wine and lime or lemon juice in a small bowl, then pour 2 tablespoons of the mixture over each piece of salmon. Drizzle the fish with the melted butter and season to taste with salt and pepper. Top each piece of salmon with a lime or lemon slice, the remaining vegetables, and 2 herb sprigs.

Fold the other half of the paper heart over the fish and tightly seal the packet by making a series of tight overlapping folds along the open edge. Place on a baking sheet and bake until the packets are puffed up, about 10 minutes. Immediately transfer packets to individual plates, garnish with the remaining herb sprigs, and serve.

Serves 6.

Leaf-Wrapped Stuffed Salmon

3 heads lettuce, preferably butter type,
    or 1 pound fresh young sorrel
    leaves

LEMON-ALMOND STUFFING
1 cup fine fresh bread crumbs,
    processed from about 3 ounces
    good-textured white bread,
    preferably French
1 cup unblanched almonds
1 cup fresh parsley sprigs
1 tablespoon fresh tarragon or
    thyme leaves
3 tablespoons freshly grated
    lemon zest
¼ cup freshly squeezed lemon juice
¼ pound (1 stick) unsalted butter,
    softened
Salt
Freshly ground black pepper
Ground cayenne pepper

1 whole 5- to 8-pound salmon, dressed
    and boned (page 11)
Salmon caviar or cooked crayfish
    for garnish (optional)

Gourmet extraordinaire Stephen Suzman shared his favorite salmon presentation. The stuffing is so good, you'll want to cook an extra batch in a baking dish or hollowed-out lemons as shown. Serve the salmon with lemon and butter or melted Composed Butter made with ginger (page 86). For individual servings, divide the stuffing and wrapping among six one-pound farm-raised fish.

Preheat the oven to 350° F.

Dip the lettuce or sorrel leaves in boiling water just until wilted, about 10 seconds. Remove immediately to a bowl of ice water, drain, and spread out on paper toweling; reserve.

To make the stuffing, combine the bread crumbs, almonds, and parsley in a food processor or blender and process just until coarsely chopped and well mixed. Add the tarragon or thyme, lemon zest and juice, and butter and mix thoroughly. Season to taste with salt, pepper, and cayenne.

Quickly rinse the salmon under running cold water and pat dry with paper toweling. To determine the cooking time, measure the fish across the back (hold the ruler perpendicular to the spine) at its widest point. Stuff the cavity of the salmon with the bread crumb mixture. Place the fish on a baking sheet. Drain the blanched lettuce or sorrel leaves and wrap the fish in the leaves, overlapping them as you work and covering the fish completely with several layers.

Bake the salmon until the flesh is barely opaque throughout, about 10 minutes per inch of thickness. Garnish with caviar or crayfish and serve immediately or at room temperature. To serve, cut the fish crosswise into 1-inch-thick slices.

Serves 6 to 12.

Baked Dill-Stuffed Fillet

Dill pickles add an unusual dimension to the stuffing of these attractive salmon rolls. Drizzle the rolls with melted butter or Beurre Blanc (page 86) before serving.

To make the stuffing, combine the bread crumbs, onion, pickle, and herbs in a bowl and mix thoroughly. Stir in the butter, light cream, and enough dill pickle juice to moisten well. Season to taste with salt and pepper. Set aside.

Preheat the oven to 375° F.

Quickly rinse the salmon under cold running water and pat dry with paper toweling. Slice the salmon into 8 equal scallops about ¼ inch thick. Place each scallop between 2 pieces of waxed paper or foil and pound very lightly to create an even thickness. Season to taste with salt and pepper. Spread each scallop with one-eighth of the stuffing mixture, roll up jelly-roll fashion, secure with a slender wooden skewer or tie closed with white cotton string, and place in a baking dish or pan.

Drizzle the melted butter over the salmon rolls. Cover the dish with foil and bake until the salmon is opaque throughout, about 30 minutes; uncover for the last 10 minutes. Remove from oven and discard the skewer or string.

Garnish the rolls with lemon slices or gherkins and dill sprigs. Serve immediately.

Serves 4 as a main course, 8 as a starter.

DILL STUFFING
2 cups fine fresh bread crumbs,
    processed from about 7 ounces
    good-textured white bread,
    preferably French
2 tablespoons minced yellow onion
⅓ cup minced dill pickle
1 tablespoon minced fresh sage, or 1
    teaspoon dried sage
1½ teaspoons minced fresh thyme,
    or ½ teaspoon dried thyme
5 tablespoons unsalted butter,
    melted
½ cup light cream (or
    half-and-half)
Dill pickle juice
Salt
Freshly ground black pepper

1 piece (about 2 pounds) salmon fillet,
    skinned
Salt
Freshly ground black pepper
2 tablespoons unsalted butter, melted
Thinly sliced lemon or tiny dilled
    gherkins for garnish
Fresh dill sprigs for garnish

Roasted Salmon

Serve this succulent salmon with Beurre Blanc (page 86), Tomato Sauce (page 93), or other favorite warm sauce for fish. Use the same technique to roast a center chunk or salmon half.

Preheat the oven to 450° F.

Quickly rinse the salmon under cold running water and dry with paper toweling. Lightly season the cavity with salt and pepper and stuff it with the herbs and lemon slices. If desired, insert small metal skewers through the edges of the cavity and lace with cotton string to keep the fish intact. To determine the cooking time, measure the fish across the back (hold the ruler perpendicular to the spine) at its widest point.

Place the salmon on a lightly oiled baking sheet. Brush the fish all over with the melted butter. Roast until the flesh is barely opaque throughout, about 10 minutes per inch of thickness.

Remove the salmon from the oven to a work area or serving platter and remove the twine and skewers, if used. Garnish and serve immediately.

Serves 6 to 12.

1 whole 5- to 8-pound salmon, pan-dressed and boned (page 11) if desired
Salt
Freshly ground black pepper
About 12 fresh herb sprigs, such as dill, fennel, oregano, or thyme
1 or 2 lemons, thinly sliced
About ¼ pound (1 stick) unsalted butter, melted
Lemon slices for garnish
Red sweet pepper strips for garnish
Fresh herb sprigs (same as above) for garnish

Herb-Roasted Salmon

2¼ pounds salmon fillet, skin intact,
    cut into 6 equal pieces
Salt
Freshly ground black pepper
3 tablespoons safflower or peanut oil
6 tablespoons (¾ stick) unsalted butter
About 2 cups mixed fresh herb sprigs,
    such as chervil, dill, fennel,
    parsley, tarragon, and thyme, in
    any combination

Serve directly from the oven with Champagne Sauce (page 89), or its red wine variation, or with Beurre Blanc (page 86).

Preheat the oven to 400° F.

Quickly rinse the salmon under cold running water and pat dry with paper toweling. Season the salmon to taste with salt and pepper.

Heat the oil in a large heavy ovenproof skillet over high heat. Add 2 or 3 of the fillets, skin side up, and sauté until lightly browned, about 1 minute; turn and sauté on the skin side about 1 minute. Using a wide spatula, remove the fish to a cutting board. With a sharp knife, cut the skin away from each fillet but leave it attached at one end. Top the skin side of each fillet with 1 tablespoon of butter and distribute about half of the herb sprigs over the fillets. Reposition the skin so that it covers the herbs and place the salmon pieces in the skillet or a baking dish. Bake until just done and opaque throughout, 6 to 8 minutes.

Remove the fillets from the oven and discard the skin and herbs. If desired, cut each piece of fillet crosswise into two equal-sized strips. Spoon about 2 tablespoons of the sauce onto each of 6 dinner plates and place a fillet or 2 strips on top. Garnish with the remaining herb sprigs. Serve immediately.

Serves 6.

Sautéed Salmon Scallops with Greens

2 pounds fresh Swiss chard, spinach,
    or other greens
2 pounds salmon fillet, skinned
Salt
Freshly ground black pepper
About ¼ pound (1 stick) unsalted
    butter
1 large yellow onion, finely chopped
2 garlic cloves, minced or pressed
1 tablespoon olive oil
3 tablespoons freshly squeezed lemon
    juice
3 tablespoons minced fresh parsley,
    preferably flat-leaf Italian type

Nestle quickly sautéed salmon in a nest of deep-green Swiss chard or other similar greens. For easier slicing, place the salmon in the freezer for about one hour before cutting.

Wash the chard or other greens thoroughly, remove tough stems, and shred leaves with a large knife. Reserve.

Quickly rinse the salmon under cold running water and pat dry with paper toweling. Slice the salmon into 8 equal scallops about ¼ inch thick. Place each piece between 2 pieces of waxed paper or foil and pound very lightly to create an even thickness. Season to taste with salt and pepper.

Heat 3 tablespoons of the butter in a sauté pan or skillet over medium-high heat. Add the onion and sauté until soft but not brown, about 4 minutes. Stir in the garlic and greens and sauté until the greens are just tender, about 3 minutes. Remove from the heat and keep warm.

Heat 2 tablespoons of the butter and the oil in the pan over medium-high heat. Sauté 3 or 4 salmon scallops at a time, cooking about 25 seconds on the first side, then turning and cooking about 15 seconds on the other side. Remove the scallops to paper toweling to drain briefly. Cook the remaining scallops in the same way, adding more butter or oil if necessary. When all the scallops are cooked, add the lemon juice to the pan and scrape the bottom of the pan with a wooden spoon to loosen browned bits. Add the remaining butter and stir until melted. Stir in the minced parsley.

To serve, divide the greens among warmed plates, top with 1 or 2 of the salmon scallops, pour the pan sauce over the scallops, and serve immediately.

Serves 4 as a main course, 8 as a starter.

GRILLED, BARBECUED, & BROILED

Mid-summer salmon, caught from the oceans and bays, are firmer and richer tasting than spring salmon and are best grilled, barbecued, or broiled. Salmon may be cooked by these methods whole, in sections sold as roasts, carved into steaks or fillets, or cut into small chunks and skewered. When grilling or barbecuing a large whole salmon, place it in a hinged wire basket for easier handling. It also looks and tastes fantastic when cooked on a revolving spit.

Be sure the grill rack is very clean, with no charred remains to which fish skin or flesh can stick, and brush it thoroughly with vegetable oil before placing the fish on it. Except for the slower barbecue method described on page 47, salmon should be cooked fast over a fairly hot fire to sear the surface quickly and prevent the fish from clinging to the rack. To reduce further the chance of sticking, position the fish perpendicular to the grill bars so there is less direct contact. Leaving the salmon in one position and turning only once during cooking also helps minimize sticking. Remove the fish from the grill *just before* it is done to your liking; it will continue to cook for a short while off the heat.

Recipes for grilling and broiling are interchangeable. To convert to broiling, just position the broiler rack five or six inches from the heat source.

INDIAN STYLE

American Indians originated the practice of skewering filleted salmon on ironwood stakes and sticking them in the ground to cook around a smoldering campfire of aromatic alder or other hardwood. It's still a great way to cook salmon at the beach or other areas free from fire hazard.

In lieu of ironwood stakes, cut ⅜-inch-round wooden dowels (available at any building supply house) into 2½-foot lengths. Whittle a sharp point on one end for sticking through the fish. Presoak the stakes in water for at least 1 hour before using (to prevent them from burning too much during the cooking). Thread the salmon onto the stakes, brush with olive oil or melted butter, and position the stakes so that the fish is about 1 foot from the fire. Turn the stakes occasionally until the fish is done on all sides.

Grilled Salmon

6 salmon steaks (about 6 ounces *each*),
    or 2¼ pounds fillet, skinned and
    cut into 6 equal pieces
Olive oil, preferably extra-virgin, or
    melted unsalted butter for
    brushing
Salt
Freshly ground black pepper

No salmon preparation beats the rich taste of grilled fish served with just a squeeze of lemon and some melted butter. To dress it up a bit more, top the cooked fish with Beurre Blanc (page 86) or a Composed Butter (page 86). Use the same method to grill whole salmon, increasing the cooking time according to the size of the fish.

Prepare a hot charcoal or wood fire in an uncovered grill.

Quickly rinse the salmon under cold running water and pat dry with paper toweling. Brush the fish all over with olive oil or melted butter and season to taste with salt and pepper. Grill the fish, turning once and basting occasionally with the oil or butter, until the flesh is just opaque, 6 to 10 minutes total cooking time, depending on thickness. Serve immediately unadorned or as suggested in the introduction.

Serves 6.

VARIATION: After brushing with olive oil or melted butter, use white cotton string to tie the salmon inside bundles of fresh dill, fennel, sage, lovage, or other herb stalks as shown on page 40.

Grilled Fennel-Stuffed Baby Salmon

4 small (1 pound *each*) whole salmon,
   dressed and boned (page 11) if
   desired
Salt
Freshly ground black pepper
1 medium-sized sweet fennel bulb, cut
   in half vertically then very thinly
   sliced
2 lemons, very thinly sliced
Olive oil, preferably extra-virgin,
   for brushing

Look for small farm-raised coho salmon. Serve the hot fish with pleasantly pungent Garlic Sauce (page 91) or a scoop of Composed Butter (page 86).

Prepare a hot charcoal or wood fire in an uncovered grill.

Quickly rinse the salmon under cold running water and pat dry with paper toweling. Season lightly with salt and pepper and stuff the fish cavities with the sliced fennel and lemon. Brush the fish all over with olive oil.

Grill the salmon, turning once, until the flesh is just opaque, about 10 minutes total cooking time. Remove from the grill to warmed dinner plates and serve immediately.

Serves 4.

Corn-Wrapped Salmon and Scallops

Grilled salmon and garden-fresh corn is an unbeatable combination of late-summer harvests. Here's an unusual presentation of the classic team. Since scallops cook in about the same time as salmon, they're perfect additions to the tasty bundles.

Prepare a hot charcoal or wood fire in an uncovered grill.

Remove the husks and silks from the corn, being careful not to tear the husks and keeping them as fully intact as possible. Remove 1 sturdy leaf from each set of husks and cut each of these lengthwise into 2 strips; reserve all the husks. Cut the corn kernels from the cobs, place in a bowl, and reserve.

Spread out the 4 sets of corn husks on a flat surface, making sure the leaves overlap to prevent leakage during cooking. Spoon one-fourth of the corn kernels in the center of each. Top the corn with a piece of salmon and one-fourth of the scallops. Sprinkle each packet with the lemon juice, green onions, and salt and pepper to taste, and dot with butter. Bring the husks together to enclose the contents completely and tie each end with a strip of husk.

Grill, turning once, until the salmon is just opaque, about 10 minutes. Test by opening one of the corn packets.

Serves 4.

VARIATION: Though certainly less picturesque, foil may be used instead of the corn husks.

4 corn ears
1 pound salmon fillet, skinned and cut
  into 4 equal pieces
1 pound small sea scallops
¼ cup freshly squeezed lemon juice
4 green onions, thinly sliced
Salt
Freshly ground black pepper
4 tablespoons (½ stick) unsalted butter

Teriyaki

4 salmon steaks (about 6 ounces *each*), skinned, or 1-1/2 pounds fillet, skinned
Teriyaki Marinade (page 85)

Broiled salmon infused with Japanese seasonings is an easy and delicious change of routine. Serve with fluffy rice, steamed spinach, and hot green tea, warm *sake*, or cold Japanese beer. It can also be cooked on the grill.

Quickly rinse the salmon under cold running water and pat dry with paper toweling. Divide each steak into 2 pieces by cutting along either side of the central bone and then discarding the bone; alternatively, cut the fillet into 8 equal pieces.

Place the salmon in a shallow glass or ceramic container and pour 1 cup of the marinade over the fish. Cover and refrigerate for 2 hours, turning the fish occasionally. Let come to room temperature before cooking.

Preheat the broiler.

Remove the salmon from the marinade, reserving the marinade. Place the fish on an oiled rack set in a baking pan. Position the fish 5 or 6 inches from the heat source and broil, turning once and brushing with the reserved marinade several times, until the flesh is just opaque, 3 to 5 minutes per side, depending on thickness. Meanwhile, heat the remaining ¾ cup marinade. Serve the salmon at once, with the heated marinade as a dipping sauce.

Serves 4.

SMOKED & CURED

*B*efore the advent of cold storage, salmon was preserved for longer life by smoking or curing in brine. Today we continue these practices strictly for the superb flavors they impart.

Ranging in price and flavor from salty lox to creamy Nova Scotia style, some form of smoked salmon is commercially available almost everywhere. More often than not, good smoked salmon is expensive; however, many excellent dishes can be made from very economical end cuts or trimmings. Vacuum-packed whole fillets are available by mail order in places where fresh or even smoked salmon is difficult to find. They're great to keep on hand for unexpected entertaining.

For economy and flavor that rivals or occasionally exceeds the best imports, smoke your own salmon whenever good-quality whole fish or fillets are readily available. Home smoking is not only kind to your budget, but also a great culinary adventure. Invite friends over for a dinner of aromatic salmon warm from the smoker or for a brunch featuring chilled salmon and the traditional condiments.

At the end of this section you'll find two delectable Scandinavian methods of curing salmon in brine and a Pacific island dish that "cooks" the fish in lime juice.

SHOPPER'S GUIDE

INDIAN STYLE: Two styles of Pacific species slow-smoked by Indians from Pacific Northwest to Alaska; one is moist and very smoky flavored; the other, sometimes called squaw candy, is cut into strips and smoked until very tough and rubbery, like beef jerky. Squaw candy needs no refrigeration, making it good for backpacking or camping.

KIPPERED: Baked during smoking; moist, tender, and flaky; no salty taste. Nonfish eaters like it. Best sliced about 1 inch thick.

LOX: The most popular preserved salmon; prepared mostly from Pacific species that are cured in brine, then soaked to remove salt; sometimes still lightly smoked after soaking as it always was in the past; inexpensive, often salty. Name derives from Scandanivan for salmon, *lax*. Buy thinly sliced on the diagonal.

NOVA SCOTIA: True Nova come only from eastern Canada; cold-smoked; expensive; creamy with very little saltiness. The term "Nova" is also commonly used to refer to any smoked salmon regardless of source; quality varies according to the salmon and the smoking process. Buy thinly sliced on the diagonal.

SCOTTISH, IRISH, and **NORWEGIAN:** Cold-smoked Atlantic salmon; superb quality; expensive; dry and delicate; not salty. Buy very thinly sliced on the diagonal.

Smoked Salmon

2 quarts water
1 cup salt
1¼ cups granulated or firmly packed
    brown sugar
3 bay leaves
2 salmon fillets (about 3 pounds *each*),
    skin intact
About 10 cups very small hickory or
    other aromatic wood chips for
    smoking

Use this method to smoke smaller pieces of salmon as well as whole fillets. Serve with cream cheese, a Composed Butter (page 86), or other favorite spread; dark bread or bagels; thinly sliced or chopped red sweet onion; and sliced tomatoes.

To make the brine, combine the water, salt, sugar, and bay leaves in a large bowl; stir well.

Quickly rinse the salmon fillets under cold running water and pat dry with paper toweling. Place the fish in a shallow glass or ceramic container and pour the brine over it to cover. Cover the container with plastic wrap and refrigerate for at least 3 or up to 10 hours, depending on thickness of fillets. Drain the salmon, rinse well in cold water, and place, skin side up and uncovered, on a wire rack until the flesh is dry, 30 minutes to 1 hour.

Preheat the smoker and add wood chips according to the manufacturer's directions. Rub the rack with vegetable oil to prevent the fish from sticking.

Place each fillet on several layers of cheesecloth or a sheet of heavy brown paper and cut the cloth or paper into the shape of the fillet. When the temperature in the smoker reaches 170° F., place each fillet, skin side down, on the cheesecloth or paper and transfer, cloth side down, to the smoker rack. Cover the smoker and smoke the fish until it is just opaque, 10 to 12 hours. Restock the wood chips whenever necessary, usually about 3 pans of chips are needed in all.

Remove the salmon from the smoker. Cool briefly, then peel off the cheesecloth or paper, which takes the skin with it. Serve immediately, or cool, cover, and refrigerate for up to 2 weeks. Or tightly wrap in freezer wrap and freeze for up to 2 months.

Serves 12 to 16.

VARIATION: Do not add sugar to the brine. Just before placing the fish in the smoker, generously baste it with pure maple syrup. Baste with more maple syrup several times during the smoking process.

Smoked Salmon Canapés

Prepare a tray of these for passing with cocktails or wine, or compose individual first-course or lunch plates accompanied with a cucumber salad punctuated with tiny radishes.

Place the cream cheese and horseradish in a bowl and whip with an electric mixer or wire whisk until light and fluffy. Stir in the minced herbs and season to taste with lemon juice and pepper. Spread on bread.

Cut the salmon slices into the same shape as the bread and place on top of the spread (fit together small salmon pieces if necessary). Garnish with dill and capers and serve immediately.

Serves 6.

8 ounces cream cheese, softened
1 tablespoon prepared white horseradish, drained
1 tablespoon minced fresh chives
1 tablespoon minced fresh dill
Freshly squeezed lemon juice
Freshly ground black pepper
About 9 thin slices rye or pumpernickel bread, cut into 18 triangles or other interesting shapes and toasted if desired
12 ounces smoked salmon, very thinly sliced on the bias
Fresh dill sprigs for garnish
Capers for garnish

Smoked Salmon Spread

8 ounces cream cheese, softened
3 tablespoons heavy (whipping) cream
5 ounces smoked salmon trimmings,
    minced
1 tablespoon minced fresh chives
    or green onion
Freshly squeezed lemon juice
Ground cayenne pepper
Freshly ground black pepper

Delicious on bagels, brioche, croissants, or French or pumpernickel bread, as well as a dip for raw vegetables, this spread is a great way to use the more economical trimmings from smoked salmon. It may be covered and refrigerated up to one day; bring to room temperature before serving.

Combine the cream cheese and heavy cream in a bowl and whip with an electric mixer or wire whisk until light and fluffy. Stir in the smoked salmon, chives or green onion, and lemon juice, cayenne, and black pepper to taste.

Serves 8 to 12.

Smoked Salmon Cream

12 ounces smoked salmon trimmings,
    chopped
1 tablespoon prepared horseradish,
    drained
Freshly ground black pepper
1 cup heavy (whipping) cream,
    whipped

Here's another good way to use those smoked salmon trimmings. The mixture can be piped onto cucumber slices and garnished with a bit of salmon caviar or a boarge flower or spread onto small pieces of toast.

Combine the salmon, horseradish, and pepper to taste in a food processor and pulse on/off until the salmon is finely minced but not smooth, about 10 seconds. Transfer to a bowl and fold in the whipped cream.

Push the mixture through a medium sieve into a bowl; scrape off any that clings to the bottom of the sieve into the bowl. Transfer to a small serving dish and chill for at least 1 hour or as long as overnight.

Serves 10 to 12 as a starter.

Smoked Salmon Pâté

¼ pound (1 stick) unsalted butter,
    softened
1 pound smoked salmon trimmings
1 cup minced or grated white sweet
    onion
1 cup minced fresh chives
Freshly squeezed lemon juice
Salt
Freshly ground black pepper

Pipe this scrumptious pâté onto crisp endive leaves or sliced apples to offer as a starter. Or serve on toasted French bread or croutons (made by frying thinly sliced bread in olive oil or butter until golden), alone or with a green salad. My friend Mary McCoy spreads this irresistible blend on whole-grain bread, tops it with cheese, broils it, and then crowns it with a dab of pesto.

Place the butter in a bowl and whip it with an electric mixer or wire whisk until light and fluffy. Set aside.

Place the salmon in a food processor and pulse on/off until well chopped. Add it to the whipped butter and stir with a wooden spoon until the fish and butter are well blended but the mixture is still slightly coarse. Stir in the onion, chives, and lemon juice, salt, and pepper to taste. Pack the mixture into a crock, cover, and refrigerate overnight to blend flavors. Served chilled or at room temperature.

Serves 6 to 8.

NOTE: To serve as shown, let the mixture soften for about 20 minutes at room temperature, then place it in a pastry bag fitted with a fluted tip and pipe onto endive leaves. Garnish with chive blossoms.

Gravlax

2 pieces salmon fillets (about 2 pounds *each*), skin intact
12 fresh dill sprigs
⅓ cup kosher (coarse) salt
¼ cup granulated sugar
1 teaspoon white peppercorns, cracked
¼ cup aquavit or Cognac (optional)

When making gravlax, the Swedes traditionally lay pine or spruce twigs in the bottom of the container before adding the fish. Though picturesque, this touch of nature is not necessary to create this succulent treat, also known as *gravad lax*. Slice the cured salmon paper-thin on the bias. Roll the slices into rosette shapes and serve with Mustard Sauce (page 85) or a Composed Butter (page 86) on toasted thinly sliced bread. Top each with a caper as shown. Or arrange the slices on a platter and garnish with fresh dill or chives and lemon or cucumber. Offer toasted bread, sauce, and capers alongside.

Quickly rinse the salmon under cold running water and pat dry with paper toweling.

Place about one-third of the dill sprigs in a flat glass or ceramic dish large enough to hold the fillets.

Combine the salt, sugar, peppercorns, and aquavit or Cognac in a bowl. Rub the fleshy side of each piece of salmon with half of the salt mixture. Place a fillet, skin side down, on top of the dill in the dish. Top with half of the remaining dill. Cover it with the other fillet, skin side up, placing thick width to thin width to create a uniform thickness. Arrange the remaining dill sprigs over the fish. Cover the dish loosely with plastic wrap and place about a 5-pound weight (such as bricks, boards, or canned foods) on top to press the fish down. Refrigerate for 3 or 4 days. Remove the weight and plastic cover 2 or 3 times each day, separate the fillets, and baste the cut sides with the juices that have accumulated in the dish. Place the fillets together again, turn them over, cover again, and reposition the weights.

To serve, remove the dill and place the fillets skin side down on a cutting board. Slice the fillets on the diagonal into thin strips, freeing them from the skin. Serve as described in the introduction.

Serves about 30 as a starter, 12 as a main course.

VARIATION: Substitute about 1 cup smoky-flavored Lapsang souchong tea leaves for the dill sprigs. Use a dull knife and paper toweling to remove the tea leaves before slicing. Serve as above.

Pickled Salmon

Warm boiled or steamed new potatoes, briefly tossed in the salmon marinade, are customarily served with this delicacy.

In a nonreactive saucepan, combine the water, vinegar, sugar, salt, onion, lemon, mustard seeds, peppercorns, and bay leaves. Bring to a boil over medium-high heat, stirring until the sugar melts. Remove from the heat and cool.

Put the fish and dill sprigs in a glass or ceramic container and pour the cooled vinegar solution over, gently stirring or shaking to coat all the pieces. Cover and refrigerate for at least 24 hours or up to 4 or 5 days.

To serve, pour off the brine (strain some and toss with warm potatoes, if using) and arrange the salmon, with the pickled onion and lemon, in a bowl. Serve with toothpicks, tiny skewers, or cocktail forks for spearing.

Serves about 30 as a starter.

1 cup water
1 cup distilled white vinegar
3 tablespoons granulated sugar
½ teaspoon salt
1 small white onion, thinly sliced, or 1 cup peeled whole tiny onions
1 lemon, thinly sliced
1 tablespoon mustard seeds
1 teaspoon black peppercorns, cracked
2 bay leaves
2 pounds salmon fillet, skinned, rinsed, dried, and cut into bite-sized pieces
¾ cup firmly packed fresh dill sprigs

Lomilomi

1 pound salmon fillet, skinned
¼ cup finely chopped red sweet onion
½ teaspoon granulated sugar
2 teaspoons salt, or to taste
Tabasco sauce
About 1 cup freshly squeezed lime
    juice (about 8 limes)
3 cups peeled, seeded, and chopped
    vine-ripened tomatoes, drained
    and chilled
¼ cup minced fresh cilantro
    (coriander)
Lime slices for garnish
Fresh cilantro (coriander) sprigs
    for garnish

Lime-macerated salmon makes a refreshing lunch or supper during sultry weather. My inspiration for this version of seviche comes from a recipe shared by cooking teacher Babs Retzer. The name is taken from the Hawaiian word for massage, which is exactly what you will do to the salmon after it cures in the lime juice.

Though it's unlikely that any parasites will be harboring in fresh salmon, a brief freezing kills any such lurkers. Serve the salmon in small bowls or shells or on crisp garden greens.

Quickly rinse the salmon under cold running water and pat dry with paper toweling. Wrap and freeze the fish until firm, about 6 hours. Thaw slightly, then cut into ½-inch dice.

Place the diced salmon in a ceramic or glass container and add the onion, sugar, salt, and several drops of Tabasco. Pour in just enough lime juice to cover. Cover and refrigerate at least 5 hours or as long as 24 hours, stirring occasionally.

Just before serving, knead the salmon mixture briefly with your fingers. Add the tomatoes and cilantro and mix well. Garnish with lime and cilantro and serve immediately.

Serves 3 or 4 as a main course, 6 as a starter.

COOKED SALMON

*T*his section features dishes that call for cooked salmon. The recipes are great ways to use leftover grilled, poached, or baked fish, though they are so good it is worth cooking salmon just to prepare them.

To ready cooked salmon for these recipes, remove the skin and large bones, pull out any tiny hidden bones with tweezers, and scrape away any gray flesh with a dull knife.

When freshly cooked salmon is unavailable, these dishes can be made, though not as successfully, with high-quality canned salmon. To use canned salmon, drain it well, then turn it into a colander and quickly dip it in cold water a couple of times to wash away the oil used in canning. Pat the fish dry with paper toweling, remove and discard skin and bones, then use in any recipe that calls for cooked salmon.

Salmon Salad Niçoise

DIJON VINAIGRETTE
¼ cup white wine vinegar
1 tablespoon Dijon-style mustard
3 garlic cloves, minced or pressed
1 teaspoon granulated sugar
Salt
Freshly ground black pepper
½ cup olive oil, preferably extra-virgin

6 small thin-skinned potatoes,
    well scrubbed
½ pound tender green beans, tips and
    strings removed, or edible pod
    peas
About 3 cups young salad greens,
    washed, dried, and chilled
4 vine-ripened Italian plum tomatoes,
    sliced, or 1 cup cherry tomatoes,
    stemmed
1 small red sweet onion, thinly sliced
    and separated into rings
3 hard-cooked eggs, peeled and
    quartered, or 12 hard-cooked
    quail eggs, peeled
3 cups flaked cold cooked salmon, or
    18 ounces cooked salmon fillet,
    cut into small pieces
¾ cup Niçoise or other oil-cured olives
Anchovy fillets for garnish (optional)
Lemon wedges for garnish (optional)

Perfect for an outdoor hot-weather lunch.

To make the vinaigrette, combine the vinegar, mustard, garlic, sugar, and salt and pepper to taste in a small bowl. Slowly whisk in the olive oil. Reserve.

Steam the potatoes until tender when pierced, about 20 minutes. Cool, slice, and reserve.

Steam the green beans or peas until crisp-tender, about 10 minutes. Cool quickly in ice water, drain, and reserve.

On individual plates, arrange the salad greens, sliced potatoes, green beans or peas, tomatoes, onion rings, eggs, salmon, and olives. Garnish with anchovies and lemon if desired. Spoon on some of the vinaigrette and serve immediately. Pass the remaining vinaigrette.

Serves 4 to 6.

VARIATION: Place all of the ingredients in separate bowls and let everyone assemble their own salads.

Salmon Mousse

Scottie McKinney, the San Francisco caterers' caterer, shared this recipe. Serve with sliced baguette or favorite plain crackers.

Combine the gelatin and water in a small saucepan, then heat over medium heat, stirring, until the gelatin dissolves. Cool slightly.

Place the salmon, onion, sour cream, mayonnaise, lemon juice, salt, Tabasco, and paprika in a blender or food processor and purée until smooth. Add the gelatin, capers, and dill and blend to mix well. Transfer to a bowl and fold in the whipped cream. Turn the mixture into a lightly oiled mold or into 12 individual molds. Refrigerate until set, at least 4 hours or as long as 12 hours.

To unmold, dip the lower part of the mold into a container of hot water for several seconds, then run a thin knife blade around the inside edges of the mold. Invert onto a serving plate, garnish with chives and caviar or flowers, and serve.

Serves about 24 as a starter, or 12 as a first course.

2 envelopes (2 tablespoons) unflavored gelatin
½ cup water
3 cups (about 18 ounces) flaked cold cooked salmon
2 tablespoons grated red onion
1½ cups sour cream
½ cup mayonnaise
3 tablespoons freshly squeezed lemon juice
1 teaspoon salt, or to taste
½ teaspoon Tabasco sauce, or to taste
¼ teaspoon sweet paprika
2 tablespoons drained capers, chopped
1 tablespoon minced fresh dill
1 cup heavy (whipping) cream, whipped
Whole fresh chives or other herbs for garnish
Salmon caviar for garnish (optional)
Pesticide-free edible flowers such as borage or nasturtium for garnish (optional)

Pasta with Salmon Cream Sauce

A simple but elegant cream sauce highlights the buttery flavor of salmon. Since the heat from the sauce and the pasta will further cook the salmon, be sure to start out with fish that is not overcooked; in fact, it is best if it is slightly underdone. Though Italian pasta purists frown at coupling fish with cheese, good Parmesan complements salmon. Small portions of this very rich dish are appropriate.

Cook the pasta in 4 quarts boiling water until *al dente,* about 12 minutes for dried and 2 minutes for fresh.

Meanwhile, melt 2 tablespoons of the butter in a sauté pan or skillet over medium heat. Add the peas and sauté until crisp-tender, about 3 minutes for fresh peas and 1 minute for thawed. Add the remaining 6 tablespoons butter and the cream, reduce the heat to low, and cook, stirring occasionally, until the butter melts. Add the salmon, ½ cup of the Parmesan, and salt, pepper, and nutmeg to taste. Simmer until the cheese melts and the salmon is heated through, about 2 minutes; do not allow to boil.

Drain the pasta and place it in a heated bowl. Pour the sauce over the pasta, add the parsley, and gently toss to mix well. Serve immediately and pass the remaining ½ cup cheese at the table.

Serves 3 or 4 as a main course, 6 as a starter.

12 ounces fresh or dried *cappellini,* linguini, *spaghettini,* or other thin pasta
¼ pound (1 stick) unsalted butter
1 cup fresh shelled petite peas or thawed frozen petite peas
1 cup heavy (whipping) cream
2 cups (about 12 ounces) flaked cooked salmon
1 cup freshly grated Parmesan cheese, preferably Parmigiano Reggiano
Salt
Freshly ground white pepper
Freshly grated nutmeg
¼ cup minced fresh parsley, preferably flat-leaf Italian type

Sautéed Salmon Cakes

⅓ cup fresh parsley leaflets
4 green onions, or 3 shallots
About 3 cups fine fresh bread crumbs,
    processed from about 10 ounces
    good-textured white bread,
    preferably French
2 eggs
2 tablespoons unsalted butter, melted
2 tablespoons mayonnaise
1 tablespoon spicy brown mustard
2 teaspoons freshly squeezed
    lemon juice
2½ cups (about 15 ounces) flaked
    cooked salmon
Salt
Freshly ground black pepper
About ½ cup vegetable oil for sautéing

While growing up my only experience with salmon was pan-fried croquettes made with canned fish, all that was available at that time in rural Louisiana. These little cakes are an update on those memories.

Serve with Red Pepper Cream (page 88), Tomato Sauce (page 93), or Rémoulade Sauce (page 92).

Combine the parsley and onions or shallots in a food processor and chop fine. Add 1½ cups of the bread crumbs, the eggs, melted butter, mayonnaise, mustard, and lemon juice. Pulse on/off several times until well mixed. Add the salmon and process briefly to combine. (Alternatively, the ingredients may be chopped by hand and mixed in a bowl.) Season to taste with salt and pepper. Cover and refrigerate for at least 30 minutes or as long as overnight.

Shape the chilled salmon mixture into 12 round or oval patties about ⅜ inch thick. Dip them in the remaining bread crumbs, patting to coat all sides completely. Let stand for 5 minutes.

Preheat the oven to warm, about 200° F., and line a baking sheet or ovenproof dish with several thicknesses of paper toweling.

Heat ¼ inch of vegetable oil in a large sauté pan or heavy skillet over medium-high heat. Sauté the patties, a few at a time, turning once, until golden and crisp on each side, 1 to 2 minutes per side. Remove with a slotted spatula to the paper-lined baking sheet and place in the oven to keep warm. Cook the remaining patties, adding more oil as needed. Serve as soon as all the patties are cooked, with the chosen sauce.

Serves 6 as a main course, 12 as a starter.

VARIATION: Form the mixture into bite-sized balls, sauté, and pass on a tray with toothpicks and a sauce for dipping.

Coulibiac

BRIOCHE DOUGH
½ cup warm (110° F. to 115° F.) milk
    or water
3 tablespoons granulated sugar
2 packages (¼ ounce *each*) active
    dry yeast
3 whole eggs
4 egg yolks
12 tablespoons (¾ cup or 1½ sticks)
    unsalted butter, softened
1 teaspoon salt
Freshly grated zest of 1 lemon
    (optional)
3 to 3½ cups unbleached all-purpose
    flour

SALMON FILLING
2 pounds cooked salmon fillet, flaked
    (about 5 cups)
¼ pound (1 stick) unsalted butter,
    melted
Freshly squeezed lemon juice
Salt
Freshly ground black pepper

CRÊPES
2¼ cups unbleached all-purpose flour
    (or up to one-fourth buckwheat
    flour)
1 teaspoon salt
4 eggs
¼ pound (1 stick) unsalted butter,
    melted
About 2 cups milk
Unsalted butter, melted, for cooking

Russian in origin, this awe-inspiring presentation features salmon encased in rich brioche dough. It looks like a very complicated production, but the various steps are spread out over two days, making the preparation manageable for a very special feast. Serve warm from the oven with melted butter, a melted Composed Butter (page 86), or sour cream.

I make the loaf with a natural form as shown. If you prefer a more controlled rectangle, fold about a 6-foot length of foil over several times to form a 4-inch high band. Butter one side very generously and wrap it, buttered side next to the dough, around the bottom of the coulibiac just before placing it in the oven. Fold over the top of the foil where the strip overlaps to keep it intact. Carefully remove the foil after the first 20 minutes of baking or when the pastry has set.

The day before serving the *coulibiac,* prepare the brioche dough.

To make the dough, combine the warm milk or water and 1 tablespoon of the sugar in a bowl, sprinkle in the yeast, and let stand in a warm place until soft and foamy, about 5 minutes.

In the bowl of a heavy-duty standing mixer, combine the whole eggs, egg yolks, butter, remaining 2 tablespoons sugar, salt, lemon zest, and the foamy yeast and mix well. Gradually add 3 cups of the flour, mixing until well blended. Insert the dough hook and knead until the dough loses its stickiness, about 5 minutes. If necessary, add the remaining flour, 1 tablespoon at a time, until the dough is smooth. Alternatively, mix the dough ingredients in a large mixing bowl, adding only 2½ cups of the flour, then turn the dough out onto a lightly floured surface and knead well with flour-dusted hands until it loses its stickiness, about 10 minutes, adding as much of the remaining flour as needed to form a smooth, elastic dough. Gather the dough into a ball, transfer to a lightly oiled bowl, and turn the dough to coat all sides with oil. Cover the bowl tightly with plastic wrap and let rise in a warm, draft-free place until doubled in bulk, about 1 to 1½ hours.

Punch the dough down, return it to the bowl, turn again to coat with oil, cover tightly with plastic wrap, and refrigerate overnight.

On the day you plan to serve the *coulibiac,* make the salmon filling by combining the flaked salmon, butter, and lemon juice, salt, and pepper to taste in a large bowl. Mix well, cover, and refrigerate.

To make the crêpe batter, sift the flour and salt into a bowl. Add the eggs, one at a time, beating well with a wire whisk or electric beater after each addition. Stir in the butter and beat in enough of the milk to form a batter with the consistency of heavy cream. Refrigerate for at least 1 hour before using.

To cook the crêpes, preheat an 8-inch round crêpe pan over medium-high heat. Brush with melted butter, then pour in about 3 tablespoons of the batter and swirl the pan to coat the bottom with a thin layer of batter; pour off any excess batter. Cook until lightly browned on one side, about 1 minute. Turn and cook the other side until lightly brown, about 45 seconds. Stack the crêpes on a plate as they are cooked. You will need 12 crêpes; extra batter allows for a few mishaps.

To make the spinach-mushroom filling, wash the spinach thoroughly, remove tough stems, and finely chop the leaves. Heat 3 tablespoons of the butter in a large sauté pan or skillet, add the spinach, parsley, and dill, and sauté over high heat until the spinach is just tender, about 3 minutes. Drain well, then turn into a large bowl. Heat the remaining 3 tablespoons of butter in the pan, add the shallot and mushrooms, and sauté until the mushrooms are tender and most of the liquid has evaporated. Add to the spinach, mix well, and season to taste with salt and pepper. Set aside to cool.

To make the rice filling, combine the rice and butter in a bowl and season to taste with salt and pepper; reserve.

SPINACH-MUSHROOM FILLING
2 pounds fresh spinach
6 tablespoons (¾ stick) unsalted butter
½ cup chopped fresh parsley
3 tablespoons chopped fresh dill,
    or 1 tablespoon dried dill
2 tablespoons minced shallot
1 pound fresh mushrooms, finely
    chopped
Salt
Freshly ground black pepper

RICE FILLING
3 cups cooked wild or brown rice
6 ounces (1½ sticks) unsalted butter,
    melted
Salt
Freshly ground black pepper

About ¼ pound (1 stick) unsalted
    butter, melted
6 hard-cooked eggs
1 egg mixed with 1 tablespoon heavy
    (whipping) cream for glazing
    dough

Remove the brioche dough from the refrigerator and let come to room temperature. Punch it down, then roll out on a lightly floured surface into a large rectangle about 16 by 21 inches and ¼ inch thick. Trim edges to form a perfect rectangle; reserve trimmings. Loosely wrap the dough rectangle around the rolling pin and transfer it to a lightly oiled baking sheet. Lay the dough flat on the baking sheet and cover it with 3 of the crêpes, overlapping them slightly and leaving a 4-inch border along the long sides of the dough and a 1-inch border at each end. Brush the crêpes with melted butter, then spread them with half of the spinach mixture. Top with half of the rice. Cover with a layer of the crêpes, brush with butter, then cover them with about half of the salmon mixture. Cut the round ends off each egg and line up the eggs end to end lengthwise down the middle of the salmon, then cover with the remaining salmon. Cover the salmon with more crêpes, brush with butter, then add the remaining rice and cover it with the remaining spinach mixture. Bring the narrow sides of the dough up from the baking sheet to cover the fillings. Moisten the edges of the dough with water and press to seal them together well. Carefully turn the roll over so that it is positioned seam side down on the baking sheet and tuck the open ends of the roll under. Cut 3 small holes along the center of the top to allow steam to escape during baking. Cut the reserved dough into leaves or other shapes and decorate the top of the *coulibiac* with them. Let stand to rise in a warm place for about 25 minutes.

Preheat the oven to 375° F.

Brush the top and sides of the dough with the egg-cream mixture. Bake until the crust is golden brown, about 45 minutes. Cover loosely with foil during baking, if necessary, to prevent excess browning.

Transfer to a wire rack to cool for about 5 minutes. Carefully cut into 1-inch-wide slices and serve.

Serves 10 to 12.

Sauces & Seasonings

*T*he subtle yet rich flavor of salmon often needs no more than a squeeze of fresh lemon. A delicate or robust sauce can, however, add interest and a welcome change of routine. Here are sauces for both hot and cold salmon presentations. Some have been suggested in the preceding recipes to go with a particular cooking method. Feel free to mix and match those that intrigue.

Also included are recipes for a basic poaching liquid and a fish stock, which add flavor to many salmon preparations.

Poaching Liquid (Court Bouillon)

2 quarts water
3 cups dry white wine
2/3 cup freshly squeezed lemon juice
    or white wine vinegar
2 small onions, quartered
3 carrots, chopped
2 celery stalks, chopped
3 or 4 fresh parsley sprigs
1 tablespoon minced fresh thyme,
    or 1 teaspoon dried thyme
1 bay leaf
2 teaspoons salt (optional)
1½ teaspoons black peppercorns,
    cracked

Combine all the ingredients in a stockpot or large saucepan and bring to a boil over medium-high heat. Reduce the heat to low and simmer, partially covered, for about 1 hour. Strain and discard the vegetables and herbs. Use liquid as directed in individual recipes.

Makes about 3 quarts, enough to poach 1 large salmon or several salmon pieces.

NOTE: To use court bouillon in an aspic, it is necessary to first clarify it. Add 1 egg white and the crushed shells of 2 or 3 eggs to the strained aspic in a saucepan. Bring to a boil over medium-high heat, then remove from the heat and let stand for 10 minutes. Slowly and carefully strain the liquid through a fine sieve lined with several layers of dampened cheesecloth.

Fish Stock (Fumet)

Keep this flavorful stock in the freezer as a base for soups or sauces.

3 pounds fish heads, bones,
    and trimmings
2 medium-sized yellow onions,
    chopped
2 celery stalks, chopped
4 or 5 fresh parsley sprigs
2 bay leaves
1 tablespoon minced fresh tarragon
    or thyme, or 1 teaspoon dried
    tarragon or thyme
Poaching Liquid (adjacent recipe)
    or equal parts water and white
    wine to cover

Wash the fish parts under cold running water, crack the heads, and place in a stockpot or large saucepan. Add all the remaining ingredients and bring to a boil over medium-high heat. Reduce the heat to low and simmer, uncovered, for about 1 hour. Use a wire skimmer to remove any foam that comes to the surface during cooking. Strain through a fine wire sieve and discard the fish, vegetables, and herbs. Use the stock as directed in individual recipes or freeze in small containers for later use.

Makes about 3 quarts.

Barbecue Sauce

Wonderful for brushing on during grilling as well as for serving with the cooked salmon.

½ pound (2 sticks) unsalted butter
2 garlic cloves, halved
¼ cup soy sauce
2 tablespoons American-style
   mustard
1 tablespoon Worcestershire sauce
2 teaspoons ketchup, or to taste

Combine all the ingredients in a saucepan over low heat and simmer until the butter is melted and the flavors are well blended, about 15 minutes.

Makes about 1¼ cups, enough for 1 medium-sized whole salmon.

Teriyaki Marinade

Heat the marinade that remains after cooking the fish and serve as a table sauce.

1¼ cups soy sauce
⅓ cup *sake* (Japanese rice wine),
   mirin (sweet Japanese cooking
   wine), or sherry
6 tablespoons granulated sugar
3 garlic cloves, minced or pressed
1 tablespoon minced or grated
   ginger root

Combine all the ingredients in a small bowl and stir until the sugar dissolves.

Makes about 1¾ cups, enough for 6 to 8 servings.

Mustard Sauce

This warm sauce is also good at room temperature with smoked salmon.

3 tablespoons unsalted butter
1 cup finely chopped sweet yellow
   or red onion
¾ cup dry vermouth or white wine
1½ cups heavy (whipping) cream
3 tablespoons Dijon-style mustard
¾ cup minced fresh chives or
   parsley, preferably flat-leaf
   Italian type
Salt
Freshly ground black pepper

Melt the butter in a saucepan over low heat. Add the onion and cook, stirring frequently, until the onion is soft but not brown, about 4 minutes. Add the vermouth or wine, increase the heat to medium, and cook, uncovered, until the liquid has evaporated, about 5 minutes. Stir in the cream and cook until reduced by about one-fourth, about 4 minutes.

Remove from the heat and stir in the mustard, chives or parsley, and salt and pepper to taste. Serve immediately or cover and let stand up to 2 hours. To reheat, place over low heat and stir constantly until warm.

Makes about 1½ cups, enough for 6 servings.

Composed Butters

Butters permeated with minced fresh herbs are simply delicious on hot salmon. For a more exotic touch, try flavoring butter with minced fresh ginger root and a little Dijon-style mustard, chopped capers and anchovy fillets, chopped pitted Niçoise olives, or a little *wasabi* (Japanese horseradish powder).

To serve as a hot sauce, melt the flavored butter in a small saucepan and pour over the salmon just before serving.

¼ pound (1 stick) unsalted butter, softened
2 tablespoons minced fresh herb of choice, such as basil, chives, cilantro (coriander), dill, or tarragon
Freshly squeezed lemon or lime juice or grated zest
Salt
Freshly ground black or white pepper

Beat the butter in a bowl with a wooden spoon or in an electric mixer, food processor, or blender until light and fluffy. Add the herb and the juice or zest, salt, and pepper to taste; mix well. Cover and chill for at least 1 hour before serving, or store up to 5 days. Or wrap tightly and freeze up to 3 months. Return almost to room temperature before serving.

Makes about ½ cup, enough for about 4 servings.

Beurre Blanc

A classic with fish.

⅓ cup minced shallots
⅓ cup dry white wine
¼ cup freshly squeezed lemon juice or white wine vinegar
½ pound (2 sticks) unsalted butter, cut into 8 equal pieces
Salt
Freshly ground black pepper

Combine the shallots, wine, and lemon juice or vinegar in a nonreactive saucepan over medium-high heat and cook until the shallots are tender but not too dark and the liquid has almost evaporated, about 6 minutes; avoid scorching the shallots.

Remove the pan from the heat and add 1 piece of the butter, stirring with a wooden spoon or wire whisk until the butter is melted. Place the pan over low heat and add the remaining butter, 1 piece at a time, stirring each time until the butter is blended into the sauce. Season to taste with salt and pepper. Serve immediately or place in a double boiler over barely simmering water for up to 30 minutes.

Makes about 1 cup, enough for about 8 servings.

VARIATION: To make *beurre rouge,* use red wine and red wine vinegar.

Hollandaise Sauce

It seems like gilding the lily to team rich salmon with this old favorite, but hollandaise served with warm poached, steamed, or baked salmon is a culinary tradition. To make the two kinds of hollandaise shown on page 19, prepare the basic recipe, then turn half of it into the avocado variation.

2 egg yolks
1½ tablespoons freshly squeezed
   lemon or orange juice
¼ pound (1 stick) unsalted butter,
   cut into 8 equal pieces
Ground cayenne pepper or freshly
   ground white pepper

In the top pan of a double boiler, beat the egg yolks with a wire whisk or wooden spoon until they are light and lemon colored. Add the lemon or orange juice and 2 pieces of the butter, place over gently simmering water, and stir rapidly with a wire whisk or wooden spoon until the butter melts. Add the remaining pieces of butter, 1 piece at a time, stirring until each melts before adding the next piece. When all the butter has been added, stir in cayenne or white pepper to taste. Serve immediately or place in a double boiler over barely simmering water for up to 30 minutes. If the sauce gets too thick or begins to curdle before serving, briskly stir in a small amount of boiling water to smooth it.

Makes about 1 cup, enough for 4 servings.

VARIATIONS: Substitute balsamic vinegar for part of or all of the lemon or orange juice.

Halve, pit, and scoop out pulp from 1 very ripe avocado. Purée in a food processor or blender until very smooth. Add the warm hollandaise sauce and blend well.

Sorrel Cream

2 cups heavy (whipping) cream
1½ cups minced or shredded fresh
   young sorrel
Freshly squeezed lemon juice
Salt
Freshly ground white pepper

Place the cream and 1 cup of the sorrel in a small saucepan over low heat and simmer until the cream is reduced by half, about 15 minutes. Push through a wire sieve to remove the discolored sorrel and collect the flavored cream in a small bowl. Stir in the remaining ½ cup sorrel and season to taste with lemon juice, salt, and pepper. Reheat and serve immediately.

Makes about 1½ cups, enough for 5 or 6 servings.

Béarnaise Sauce

1½ teaspoons minced shallot or
    green onion
1½ teaspoons minced fresh
    tarragon, or ½ teaspoon dried
    tarragon
2 tablespoons white wine vinegar
2 egg yolks, well beaten
1½ tablespoons freshly squeezed
    lemon juice
¼ pound (1 stick) unsalted butter,
    cut into 8 equal pieces
Salt
Freshly ground black pepper

Combine the shallot or green onion,
tarragon, and vinegar in a small
saucepan over medium heat and cook
until very thick, almost a glaze, about
5 minutes. Cool slightly.

Place the egg yolks in the top pan of
a double boiler and beat with a wire
whisk or wooden spoon until light and
lemon colored. Add the shallot
mixture, lemon juice, and 2 pieces of
the butter, place over gently
simmering water, and stir rapidly until
the butter melts. Add the remaining
pieces of butter, 1 piece at a time,
stirring until each melts before adding
the next piece. When all the butter
has been added, stir in salt and pepper
to taste. Serve immediately or place in
a double boiler over barely simmering
water for up to 30 minutes. If the sauce
gets too thick or begins to curdle
before serving, briskly stir in a small
amount of boiling water to smooth it.

**Makes about 2 cups, enough for
about 8 servings.**

Red Pepper Cream

4 red sweet peppers
2 cups heavy (whipping) cream
Salt
Ground cayenne pepper

Roast the peppers over charcoal or gas
flame or place under a broiler, turning
several times, until the skin is charred
all over. Place in a loosely closed paper
bag to cool for about 10 minutes. Rub
away charred skin with fingertips. Cut
peppers in half, seed, devein, and
coarsely chop.

In a saucepan, combine the peppers
and cream over medium heat and cook
until the cream is reduced by half,
about 8 minutes. Transfer to a food
processor or blender and purée until
smooth. Season to taste with salt and
cayenne pepper. Return to saucepan
and reheat over low heat before
serving.

**Makes about 1½ cups, enough for
4 to 6 servings.**

VARIATION: Instead of roasted red
peppers, grill or broil 4 or 5 large vine-
ripened tomatoes just until soft, then
peel, seed, and chop them. Add to the
cream and finish as above.

Horseradish and Garlic Cream

1 1-inch piece fresh horseradish, grated or finely chopped, or 2 teaspoons prepared white horseradish, drained, or to taste
5 garlic cloves, chopped
1½ cups light cream (or half-and-half)
½ cup heavy (whipping) cream
Salt
Freshly ground white pepper

In a saucepan, combine the horseradish, garlic, and light and heavy creams over low heat and simmer until the garlic is very tender and the cream is reduced by half, about 15 minutes. Strain through a fine wire sieve into a clean saucepan. Season to taste with salt and pepper. Reheat gently and serve immediately.

Makes about 1 cup, enough for 3 or 4 servings.

Champagne Sauce

3 cups brut champagne or other sparkling wine
½ cup minced shallots
1½ cups Fish Stock (page 84)
3 cups heavy (whipping) cream
6 tablespoons (¾ stick) unsalted butter, cut into 6 equal pieces
¼ cup chopped or shredded fresh basil
Freshly squeezed lemon juice
Salt
Ground cayenne pepper

Combine the champagne or sparkling wine and shallots in a small saucepan over medium-high heat and boil until the liquid is reduced to about 3 tablespoons, about 20 minutes. Add the fish stock and continue boiling until slightly reduced, about 5 minutes. Add the cream and continue boiling until reduced to about 1¾ cups, about 7 to 8 minutes. Reduce the heat to low and add the butter, 1 piece at a time, stirring with a wooden spoon or wire whisk until each piece melts before adding the next one. When all the butter has been added, stir in the basil and lemon juice, salt, and cayenne pepper to taste. Serve immediately.

Makes about 2 cups, enough for about 8 servings.

RED WINE VARIATION: Use a light but intense red wine such as a pinot noir instead of the champagne. Add about ½ cup chopped fresh mushrooms along with the shallots, and substitute a combination of fresh fennel tops and tarragon for the basil.

Mayonnaise

Food processors or blenders make excellent mayonnaise in a flash.

1 whole egg, at room temperature
1 egg yolk, at room temperature
1 teaspoon Dijon-style mustard
1½ tablespoons freshly squeezed
    lemon juice, or to taste
1 cup safflower or other vegetable
    oil
Salt

In a blender or food processor, combine whole egg, egg yolk, mustard, and lemon juice. Blend for about 30 seconds. With the motor running at high speed, add the oil in a slow, steady stream. When mayonnaise thickens to correct consistency, turn motor off. With a rubber or plastic spatula, scrape down oil from sides of container and blend into mayonnaise. Taste and add salt and more lemon juice, if desired. Chill and serve or transfer to a covered container and refrigerate up to 5 days.

Makes about 2 cups, enough for 8 servings.

VARIATION: For Italian *maionese,* omit mustard and substitute olive oil for the safflower or vegetable oil.

Herbed Mayonnaise

While nothing beats the fresh taste of homemade mayonnaise, this herb-flavored variation, sometimes known as Green Mayonnaise, can also be very good when made with quality commercial mayonnaise that's refreshed with a squeeze of lemon juice. Use only one herb or a combination that you find complementary. Basil, dill, and tarragon impart their unique flavors and should be used alone or in combination with milder herbs such as chervil or parsley. Tender greens such as watercress or young spinach leaves are also good additions.

You may need to make two batches or double the recipe if using to mask a large poached salmon.

2 cups mayonnaise, preferably
    homemade
1 tablespoon freshly squeezed
    lemon juice, if using
    commercial mayonnaise
½ to 1 cup minced fresh herbs or
    greens

Place the mayonnaise in a bowl. If using commercial mayonnaise, stir in the lemon juice. Add the herbs and mix well with a wooden spoon or wire whisk. Transfer to a covered container and refrigerate for at least 2 hours before serving, or store up to 5 days.

Makes about 2 cups, enough for 8 servings.

Garlic Sauce (Aïoli)

This classic Mediterranean sauce is excellent with cold or hot salmon.

8 garlic cloves
2 egg yolks, at room temperature
¼ teaspoon Dijon-style mustard
1½ tablespoons freshly squeezed
    lemon juice
3 tablespoons hazelnut oil
    (optional)
1 cup olive oil, preferably extra-
    virgin, or 1 cup plus 3
    tablespoons olive oil if hazelnut
    oil is not used
Salt
Freshly ground white pepper

In a blender or food processor, mince the garlic. Add the egg yolks, mustard, and lemon juice and blend for about 30 seconds. With the motor running at high speed, slowly drizzle in hazelnut and olive oils and blend until a thick, mayonnaiselike consistency forms. Turn the motor off. With a rubber or plastic spatula, scrape down oil from sides of container and blend into the sauce. Add salt and pepper to taste. Use immediately or transfer to a covered container and refrigerate up to 2 days. Return to room temperature before serving; whisk to blend if the sauce separates.

Makes about 2 cups, enough for 8 servings.

Sour Cream Sauce

Cold salmon tastes marvelous paired with this refreshing sauce. If you're cutting calories, prepare the sauce with one cup unflavored low-fat yogurt in place of both the sour cream and mayonnaise.

½ cup sour cream
½ cup mayonnaise
1½ teaspoons Dijon-style mustard
1½ tablespoons minced fresh chives
¼ cup minced fresh dill
Freshly squeezed lemon juice
Salt
Freshly ground black or white
    pepper

Combine the sour cream or yogurt, mayonnaise, and mustard in a small bowl and blend until smooth. Stir in the minced herbs and season to taste with lemon juice, salt, and pepper. Transfer to a covered container and refrigerate for at least 1 hour before serving, or store up to 5 days.

Makes about 1½ cups, enough for 5 servings.

VARIATION: Add ¼ cup peeled, seeded, and grated cucumber to the sauce.

Rémoulade Sauce

A French tradition with cold fish.

2 cups mayonnaise, preferably
    homemade
2 teaspoons dry mustard, or to taste
2 or 3 garlic cloves, minced or
    pressed
1 tablespoon minced gherkins
1 tablespoon drained capers,
    chopped
1½ tablespoons minced fresh
    parsley
1 tablespoon minced fresh tarragon
3 anchovy fillets, minced, or
    1 teaspoon anchovy paste

Combine all ingredients in a bowl and
mix thoroughly. Transfer to a covered
container and refrigerate for at least 2
hours before serving, or store as long
as 4 days.

**Makes about 2½ cups, enough for
10 servings.**

Ravigote Sauce

For a zesty accent, try this robust
sauce with chilled salmon or pour
it over fish hot from the grill or
oven.

1 small red sweet onion, coarsely
    chopped
1 teaspoon chopped shallot or garlic
2 tablespoons chopped fresh parsley
2 tablespoons chopped fresh chives,
    chervil, dill, or tarragon
1 tablespoon drained capers, or
    to taste
1 tablespoon Dijon-style mustard,
    preferably whole grain
2 tablespoons white wine vinegar
¼ cup olive oil, preferably
    extra-virgin
Salt
Freshly ground black pepper

In a food processor or blender,
combine the onion, shallot or garlic,
herbs, capers, mustard, and vinegar
and blend until finely minced, about
10 seconds. With the motor running
at high speed, pour in the oil in a slow,
steady stream and blend until a thick,
mayonnaiselike consistency forms.
Turn off the motor. With a rubber or
plastic spatula, scrape down oil from
sides of container and blend into
sauce. Season to taste with salt and
pepper. Use immediately or transfer
to a covered container and refrigerate
up to 24 hours.

**Makes about 1 cup, enough for 4
servings.**

Tomato Sauce

A sauce of flavorful tomatoes enlivened with onion, garlic, and basil perks up late-summer grilled or baked salmon. Don't make this recipe with tasteless supermarket varieties.

3 tablespoons olive oil
1½ cups chopped yellow onion
3 garlic cloves, minced or pressed
3 pounds vine-ripened tomatoes, preferably Italian plum, peeled, seeded, and chopped
2 tablespoons shredded fresh basil
1 tablespoon minced fresh thyme, or 1 teaspoon dried thyme
1 bay leaf
Salt
Freshly ground black pepper

Heat the oil in a sauté pan or wide saucepan over medium-low heat. Add the onion and sauté until it is soft, about 4 minutes. Stir in the garlic and cook 1 minute. Add the tomatoes, herbs, and salt and pepper to taste. Simmer until the liquid reduces and the sauce is thick, about 20 minutes. Discard the bay leaf and serve the sauce. Or cool, cover, and refrigerate up to 2 days. Reheat over low heat before serving.

Makes about 3 cups, enough for about 6 servings.

Lemon Aspic

This glossy coating can be made with white wine, clear spirits such as gin or vodka, or champagne instead of the lemon juice.

2 envelopes (2 tablespoons) unflavored gelatin
2 cups clarified Poaching Liquid (page 84) or water
1 cup freshly squeezed lemon juice
Salt (optional)

Combine the gelatin and 1 cup of the Poaching Liquid or water in a small saucepan and let stand until the gelatin is soft, about 5 minutes. Place over medium heat and stir until the gelatin dissolves, about 2 minutes. Remove from the heat and add the remaining 1 cup liquid or water, the lemon juice, and salt to taste. Nest the pan in a bowl of ice or place in the refrigerator until the aspic thickens to the consistency of honey, occasionally stirring gently to prevent air bubbles from developing. The aspic can be remelted and chilled if it stiffens too much while you are working with it.

Makes about 3 cups, enough to coat 1 large whole salmon.

General Index

Atlantic salmon 5, 7

Baked salmon 27-33, 53
Barbecued salmon 47
Blueback salmon, see Sockeye
Boning 11
Broiled salmon 41

Canned salmon 5, 6, 7, 69
Catching 8
Caviar 9
Chinnok species 6
Cholesterol 6
Chum species 7
Cleaning 8
Coho species 6
Cooking time 11
Cured salmon 5, 53-66
Cutting up 10

Dog salmon, see Chum
Dogs, danger to 8
Doneness, testing for 11
Dressed 9

Farm-raised salmon 5
Fillets, cutting 10
Freezing 10
Fresh-frozen 10

Gravlax 62
Grilled salmon 41-50

Humpbacked salmon, see Pink

Indian style 41, 53
Irish salmon 7, 53

King salmon, see Chinnok
Kippered salmon 53

Life cycle 5
Lox 53

Norwegian salmon 7, 53
Nova Scotia salmon 5, 7, 53

Oils, healthy 6
Omega-3 oil 6

Pacific salmon 5, 6-7
Pan-dressed 9, 10
Parasites in raw salmon 8, 66
Pink species 7
Poached salmon 13-18
Poaching liquid 84

Raw salmon 8, 66
Red salmon, see Sockeye
Roasted salmon 27, 35-36
Roe 9

Sauces 83-93
Sautéed salmon 27, 38, 76
Scottish salmon 7, 53
Season for salmon 5
Shopping tips 9
Silver salmon, see Coho
Smoked salmon 5, 53-60
Sockeye species 6
Spawning 5
Species 6-7
Spring salmon, see Chinnok
Squaw candy 53
Steaks, cutting 10
Steamed salmon 13, 20
Stock 84
Storing 10
Strips, smoked 53

Thawing 10

Recipe Index

Aïoli, see Garlic Sauce
Aspic, Lemon 93

Baked Dill-Stuffed Fillet 33
Barbecued Salmon 47
Barbecue Sauce 85
Béarnaise Sauce 88
Beurre Blanc 86
Brioche Dough 78

Cakes, Sautéed Salmon 76
Canapés, Smoked Salmon 57
Champagne Sauce 89
Cold Poached Whole Salmon 16
Composed Butters 86
Corn-Wrapped Salmon and Scallops 49
Coulibiac 78-81
Court Bouillon, see Poaching Liquid
Crêpes 78

Dijon Vinaigrette 70
Dill Stuffing 33

Fish Stock 84
Fumet, see Fish Stock

Garlic Sauce 91
Gravlax 62
Grilled Fennel-Stuffed Baby Salmon 44
Grilled Salmon 42

Herbed Mayonnaise 90
Herb-Roasted Salmon 36
Hollandaise Sauce 87
Horseradish and Garlic Cream 89

Leaf-Wrapped Stuffed Salmon 30
Lemon Aspic 93
Lomilomi 66

Mayonnaise 90
Mousse, Salmon 73
Mustard Sauce 85

Parchment-Wrapped Salmon 28
Pasta with Salmon Cream Sauce 75
Pâté, Smoked Salmon 60
Pickled Salmon 65
Poached Fillet or Steaks 18
Poaching Liquid 84

Ravigote Sauce 92
Red Pepper Cream 88
Rémoulade Sauce 92
Rice Filling 79
Roasted Salmon 35

Salad Niçoise, Salmon 70
Salmon and Corn Chowder 23
Salmon Bisque 24
Salmon Filling 78
Salmon Mousse 73
Salmon Salad Niçoise 70
Sauces 85-93
Sautéed Salmon Cakes 76
Sautéed Salmon Scallops with Greens 38
Smoked Salmon 54
Smoked Salmon Canapés 57
Smoked Salmon Cream 58
Smoked Salmon Pâté 60
Smoked Salmon Spread 58
Sorrel Cream 87
Soups 23-24
Sour Cream Sauce 91
Spinach-Mushroom Filling 79
Steamed Salmon 20
Stuffing 30

Teriyaki 50
Teriyaki Marinade 85
Tomato Sauce 93

ACKNOWLEDGMENTS

To Jack Jensen at Chronicle Books for suggesting this book in the first place. And to the rest of the Chronicle staff for their varied and valued contributions.

To friends who shared recipes, ideas, props, and offered encouragement along the way, especially John Carr, Judi Henderson, Louis Hicks, Ken and Christine High, Douglas Jackson, Mark Leno, Mary Val McCoy, Scottie McKinney, Stephen Marcus, Marian May, Gordon and Joann Morse, Jack Porter, Babs Retzer, and Stephen Suzman.

To Tony Friscia of A. Friscia Sea Foods, San Francisco, for procuring specimen fresh salmon for photography.

To my favorite photographer Patricia Brabant for translating a host of diverse ideas into a consistent and stunning visual statement. And to her assistant Sheryl Scott for all the aid and *caffe latte.*

To the gang at The Rockpile Press—Addie Prey, Buster Booroo, Joshua J. Chew, and Michael T. Wigglebutt—who, along with Nelson Brabant, overindulged in salmon during the production of this volume.

And as always to my partner and friend Lin Cotton who makes life, with or without salmon, a feast.